House
Gymnastics

House
Gymnastics

Harrison and Ford

EBURY
PRESS

1 3 5 7 9 10 8 6 4 2

First published 2003 by Ebury Press,
An imprint of Random House,
20 Vauxhall Bridge Road, London SW1V 2SA

Random House Australia (Pty) Limited
20 Alfred Street, Milsons Point, Sydney,
New South Wales 2061, Australia

Random House New Zealand Limited
18 Poland Road, Glenfield, Auckland 10, New Zealand

Random House South Africa (Pty) Limited
Endulini, 5a Jubilee Road, Parktown 2193, South Africa

The Random House Group Limited Reg. No. 954009

www.randomhouse.co.uk

Printed and bound in Great Britain by Scotprint, Haddington

A CIP catalogue record for this book is available from the British Library.

Designed by seagulls
Illustrations by Harrison and Ford
Pictures on page 141 © John Wright

ISBN 0 09189 601 0

The authors would like to thank

Fiona, Sharmila, Lindsey, Princess Charlie, Jim and Theresa (for letting us and many a film crew climb around their house), Rob and Sue, Joan and Tom, Clizza, Bruce, Will, Rick Broadhead, Rob Glass, the inventor of the Venetian blind, Mr Goodfellow and Stina, Ben and Jess, and everyone we've met along the way. Thanks for putting up with us.

Contents

In the Beginning

House Gymnastics originated from the endeavours of Harrison and Ford in a joint and convoluted attempt to put up a bedroom blind. A perfectly good ladder was available in the basement, but Harrison and Ford took it upon themselves to install the blind without the use of any conventional aids. Using their feet and backs for leverage, they took it in turns to wedge themselves into the window frame and attempt to screw the plastic blind in place. At times, they even tried standing on each other to try to add support and ease the process. It

took almost an entire day to fit the blind, but the satisfaction gained from these alternative installation methods incited the pair to climb other things around the house and to name some of these newfound 'moves'.

Moves were being created on an almost daily basis. Everything was meticulously recorded as the house became a laboratory for the development of new moves. The naming of each new move became as important as the move itself. Language was appropriated to compliment the physical nature of House Gymnastics and let the participants communicate while performing. The hallway was renamed 'The Arena' as it became the main focus of Harrison and Ford's exploits, and words such as

Moves – House Gymnastics manoeuvres and elevated positions

- The Arena – the hallway of our house where most moves can be performed

- Busted – this phrase means that a move has been performed successfully

- Stacked it – this phrase means that a move has been performed unsuccessfully

- Do you wanna bust some moves? – Would you like to perform House Gymnastics?

- I'm amped! – I'm excited in anticipation of performing some manoeuvres

'busted' and 'amped' entered the house vocabulary as part of everyday speech (see above for brief glossary).

House Gymnastics is an art-sport that has created a global community of like-minded domestic space-embracers. The internet became a natural medium through which the word of House Gymnastics spread. Soon after the website (www.housegymnastics.com) went online, we started receiving e-mails from all over the world, spawning a global community of House Gymnasts. Every time a new move was invented and photographed, it was sent to everyone on the House Gymnastics mailing list, which was growing virally by the day through friends and friends of friends, students and bored office workers.

People were asking us for advice and help doing the moves, and e-mailing pictures of themselves doing what they'd seen us do on the site. One of the early surprise e-mails was from an American father who submitted a picture of his two-year-old son doing a handstand on the toilet!

The website is the first port of call for any would-be House Gymnast. It is constantly updated and the members list grows longer by the day. It acts as a portal for showcasing images, initiating communication and signing up new members.

Members are one of the core elements of House Gymnastics – they help to develop House Gymnastics in ever more creative ways. Potential House Gymnasts can sign up to be members on the website by filling in a simple online form. Once signed up, the rookie House Gymnast is assigned a member number and their details are listed on the site, along with the option of submitting a photo so they can parade their House Gymnastics skills to others. As well as images, members are encouraged to send in their House Gymnastics stories. One of the first and best stories came from member number 037, Mike Kinney, who hails from Massachusetts in the USA.

So, I'm sitting at the computer, checking out www.house gymnastics.com, and there's a knock on the door. I open it up, and floating there is my old buddy Satan. He was in the area doing some publicity shoots and asks if he can crash at my place. One doesn't usually go against the will of the ruler of the underworld, so I let him in. Once inside he says something about possessing nerd souls over the internet, and promptly commandeers my computer. He sees the House Gymnastics site and gets really excited, forgetting about the nerd souls. I'm not sure if anyone else has seen Lucifer all giddy and excited before, but all I can say is that he looks damn weird. He tries to do some of the moves, but his hooves and tail severely impede his progress. Then he gets this GREAT idea. He turns to me, and in his booming voice, he says, 'Yo, Mike. Let me use YOUR lithe, sexy body. It won't hurt.' I'm like, 'Hell, no!' He appreciates the irony, but being Satan he just takes over my body anyway. So, he's going around my house doing Y Chromosomes and all sorts of crazy stuff, when he realizes that no one can see how cool he is for doing this stuff. So he asks my sister to take a few pictures of him. My sister gets really creeped out by Satan for  *some reason, and doesn't want to do it, but he's threatened to consume her in fire if she doesn't, so she's quick to oblige. So, there I am, with Satan chillin' in my body, doing an X-door, screaming something about 'the day of reckoning'. Whatever that is.*

Harrison and Ford have received many amazing pictures from people signing up to become House Gymnastics members, a selection of which can be seen on the following pages.

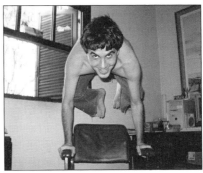

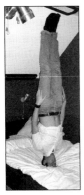

People connect with House Gymnastics because it reminds them of their childhood, when, out of a desire to be like one of their wall-climbing heroes, Batman or Spiderman, they used to climb around the house and explore. House Gymnastics allows you to enjoy your home in new and exciting ways. When someone performs House Gymnastics they become both artist and art, creating ephemeral human sculptures that last for only three seconds.

Built around an original core 25 moves that are ever increasing, it can be practised by anyone, at any time, anywhere. A crossbreed of yoga, break-dancing, climbing and gymnastics enacted in a domestic setting, moves must be held in position for three seconds to be valid. Once the key moves have been mastered indoors, they can be performed in endless outdoor situations and spaces: pubs, trees, lamp posts, elevators, public toilets, strip clubs, hotels and offices.

Although the history of House Gymnastics is brief, many benefits have been discovered. The most obvious advantage of House Gymnastics is being able to exercise in your own home without needing to buy any equipment. In a similar way to Feng Shui, House Gymnastics also brings a dynamic, creative energy into the home. Other benefits include: improvement in general fitness, greater upper body strength, increased flexibility and coordination, connection with your domestic space and, above all, the ability to impress your friends.

House Gymnastics is fun, addictive and contagious. When you see it, you will feel compelled to give it a try. Some might say 'stroke of genius', others might say, 'stop climbing around the house and get a job'.

Whatever your thoughts about House Gymnastics, we hope this book is an enjoyable read, and that it may eventually convince you to squeeze yourself upside down into your fridge or climb a massive poly-resin goose (more about that later).

Preparation

House Gym comprises 25 core moves and subsequent moves that have been submitted and chosen as Move of the Month on www.housegymnastics.com (see Moving On chapter, page 135). There are also challenges and performances, invented to test and push House Gymnasts ever forward. Some moves are a lot more difficult than others, or require specific strengths, so start with easy ones and work your way up. The moves have been divided into three sections: beginner, intermediate and expert. Each manoeuvre is also individually graded for difficulty using a star-rating system: one star being the easiest and five stars indicating the most difficult moves. The names given to the moves can be a literal translation of their visual appearance, or a reference to something that influenced the move.

Preparation is very important to House Gymnastics. If all instructions are followed carefully, injuries can be easily avoided. But if the locations

Tips

- Do not attempt whilst inebriated
- Do not attempt on a full stomach
- Always dress in loose attire
- Choose appropriate footwear (or go barefoot)
- Respect other people's homes
- Remove breakable/fragile objects
- Check sturdiness of structures
- Always warm up properly
- Perform some stretching exercises
- Have a spotting partner with you
- Stay focused
- Think of the aesthetic of the moves
- Remember to carry a notepad, pen and camera to document everything so you can share your moves with other House Gymnasts

Additional note on documentation

When recording moves it is usually necessary to have a partner present to operate the camera equipment, be it digital, 35mm SLR or a disposable camera. Although, obviously, it is possible to take the photograph yourself using a timer device, you will need to plan the move beforehand and be agile enough to get into position before the shutter is triggered. Things to consider when taking the photo include lighting, composition and scale. If possible, use a tripod to give the photo extra sharpness and quality. Lighting a shot can be done using either natural light, flash or a mixture of both. Experiment to see what works best, but remember that lower light levels without the use of a flash can increase the possibility of blurred images. Composition is important because it gives the image balance and can create an interesting aesthetic. Scale is also a key element if an image involves a lot of height, as with a Jumping Jack Wedge (see page 67). In this case the photo would need to show the floor to give a sense of the height involved.

are not properly surveyed and checked for sturdiness, or if you have not warmed up and stretched properly, injuries are likely to occur.

House Gymnastics is a spectator sport as well as a competitive one. Groups of people are always more fun and can help each other in terms of encouragement and taking turns to be each other's spotting partners. A spotting partner to act as a trouble-shooter, support, or rescuer is essential and House Gymnastics should never be attempted alone.

Warming Up

Warming up before a House Gymnastics session is an essential requirement. It loosens your muscles and gets you amped up ready for busting some moves. Five minutes of cardiovascular exercise is the minimum amount recommended.

Stretching is also recommended. Sufficient warming up and loosening of the muscles should be carried out before these stretches are attempted. Stretches must be held for approximately 20 seconds and bouncing should be avoided as this can result in strains.

The following four stretches are basic for the needs of an all-round House Gymnast. They help to stretch and warm up the fundamental muscles needed for House Gymnastics.

Types of domestic warm-up exercises:

● Step up and down stairs
● Chin-ups on a door frame
● Bicep curls using cans of baked beans
● Lift the sofa up and down
● Run in a circle around the lounge
● Do star jumps in the hall
● Perform dips using the coffee table for support
● Lunges, with a thick Stephen Hawking book in each hand (preferably hardback versions)

Chest Stretch

Stand tall, feet slightly wider than shoulder-width apart, knees slightly bent. Hold your arms out to the side, parallel with the ground and with the palms of your hands facing forward. Stretch the arms back as far as possible; you should feel the stretch across your chest. This also stretches your biceps.

Upper Back Stretch

Stand tall, feet slightly wider than shoulder-width apart, knees slightly bent. Interlock your fingers and push your hands as far away from your chest as possible, allowing your upper back to relax. You should feel the stretch between your shoulder blades.

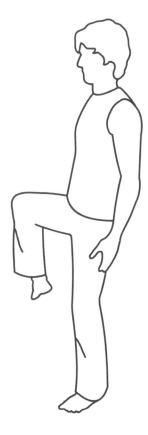

Groin Stretch

Stand tall, feet slightly wider than shoulder-width apart. Raise one knee in front of you, to groin height. Balancing on one leg (use a wall for support if needed) move knee out to side of body as far as possible. Keep spine straight and be careful not to overbalance. Repeat with the other leg.

Calf Stretch

Stand with one leg in front of the other, with the front leg bent and the back leg straight. Place hands on knee of bent leg to stabilise. Repeat with the other leg.

Checking Structures

It is always good to check structures for sturdiness. This is because the objects/structures could be weak and collapse whilst you're performing, thus leading to injury. Some well-known domestic fittings that have been found to be weak on occasion are banisters, coat rails, door frames, worktops and shelving. If a structure is found to be unsafe, repair/reinforce it, or get a spotting partner to brace the structure.

Another possible danger that can be avoided when using bare feet, is in relation to the wall surface. It is well known that bare feet can give good traction, but this is not always the case. If the wall has been painted with a vinyl-silk or eggshell finish, sweaty feet can make the surface very slippery. This can be remedied by either keeping a towel to hand to dry the undersides of feet when needed, or by dusting hands and feet with climbing chalk to absorb perspiration.

Spotting Partners

Spotting partners are very important because they can spur you on, brace structures, as well as help you down from moves or even stop you from injuring yourself if a move goes wrong. The diagrams on the next spread depict a couple of classic spotting partner situations.

Spotting a Spiderman (the spotter can help guide the performer into position and is ready to catch him or cushion his fall if he loses his grip).

Spotting an Armchair Handstand (the spotter is holding down the chair so that it remains stationary and stable for the performer).

How Not To Damage Stuff

- Trainers give good grip but can leave marks. Badminton or tennis shoes are a good choice if you don't want to mark the walls.

- If using bare feet, wipe any dirt and skank from the soles to avoid dirtying the walls. Wash hands as well.

- Move breakables out of the way.

- Take down all paintings and framed pictures from the walls.

- Test structures for strength.

- Have a spotting partner to brace the weak structures.

- Don't jar or bounce when getting into a position – move smoothly and glide.

- Distribute body weight evenly when holding a position, so as not to put unnecessary pressure on a certain object/structure.

All of the moves in the book are obviously tailored to and were worked out on the exact shape and layout of the house in Nottingham – a late-Victorian, three-up-two-down, high-ceiling terraced property in an unprepossessing area. As houses can differ radically in shape and size, the moves should be viewed as general inspiration rather than exact instructions. Some of the moves may not be possible at all in other homes. As such, the following pages are as much to help House Gymmers to adapt their own versions of the moves to suit their own location. And, of course, as simple entertainment for those who have no intention of leaving their couch and redefining their living space.

Beginner

Shelf Pirouette

Climb up onto a shelf or window sill and then swivel body outwards whilst extending a leg and an arm.

1 Stand facing a medium-sized window.

2 Raise one leg and place foot on window sill. Raise hands and place on sides of window frame.

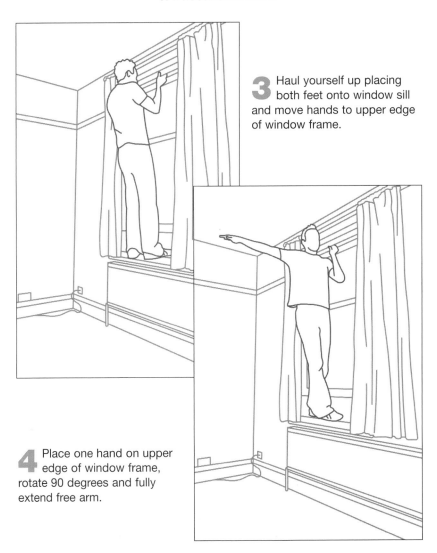

3 Haul yourself up placing both feet onto window sill and move hands to upper edge of window frame.

4 Place one hand on upper edge of window frame, rotate 90 degrees and fully extend free arm.

5 With one foot on sill, extend free leg out as far as possible.

NB. The putting up of a blind directly inspired this move. These instructions are specific to the window sill version.

Bridge

Using feet and hands as supports, with head facing upwards, form a bridge in the air between two objects/surfaces (the further apart the supports, the better the move).

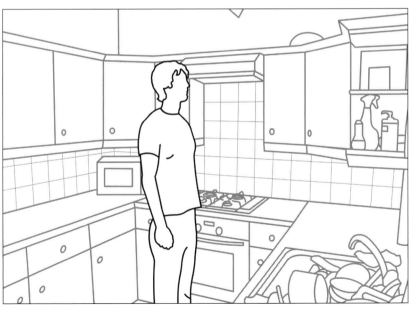

1 Stand between two large items of furniture or elevated surfaces.

2 Reaching behind yourself, place hands onto edge of surface.

3 Place one foot onto opposite surface.

4 Position other foot alongside first.

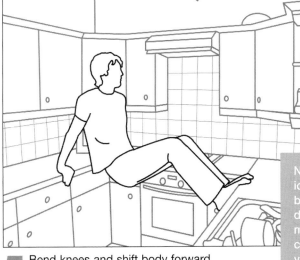

5 Bend knees and shift body forward.

NB. This move is ideal for beginners because it is simple, does not require much strength and can be performed in various locations throughout the home.

The Hang

Use any ledge around the home and hang from it.

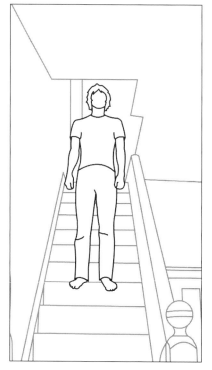

1 Stand below a ledge within reaching distance.

2 Stretch up and grasp ledge with both hands.

3 Slowly lift feet from ground bending at the knees.

4 Pull yourself up using arms and raise knees towards chest.

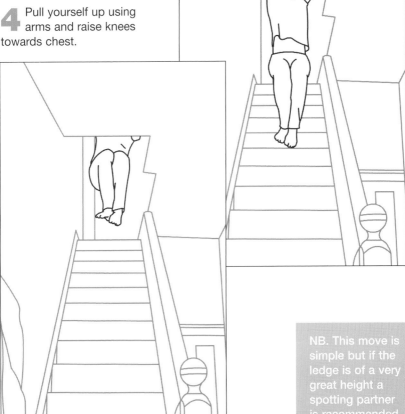

NB. This move is simple but if the ledge is of a very great height a spotting partner is recommended.

Banister Balance

Balance all of body weight across the banister without using the wall or floor for support.

★ ★ ☆ ☆ ☆

1 Stand sideways on some stairs, facing a sturdy banister.

2 Leaning forwards, grasp the banister rail with both hands a shoulder-width apart.

3 Lean further forwards to rest lower stomach area on banister.

4 Carefully tilt and shift entire weight onto the banister so that your feet become raised from the ground. Balance yourself so that the move can be held.

NB. For the move to be valid, your feet must not be touching any surrounding walls. Be carefully not to overbalance as this could result in injury – spotting partner essential as always.

Elevated Dog Stretch

*The classic yoga move elevated to a high position
(this move could be interpreted as an inverted bridge,
but the legs must be straight and parallel to the floor).*

★ ★ ☆ ☆ ☆

 Stand between two large items
of furniture or elevated surfaces,
one higher than the other.

2 Face lower surface and place hands onto it, a shoulder-width apart.

3 Put one foot onto a lower foothold behind.

4 Place second foot alongside first, raising body off floor.

5 Position one foot onto higher surface.

6 Finally, with both feet on higher surface, straighten legs so they are parallel to floor.

NB. If performing in a kitchen environment between two work surfaces, ensure that the surfaces are dry and free from dirty pans and cups.

Staircase Handstand

*A basic handstand incorporating
the stairs and an adjacent wall.*

★ ★ ☆ ☆ ☆

1 Stand next to or
on a set of stairs.

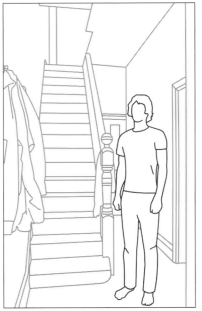

2 Bend down and grasp a
step with both hands.

3 Position one foot on an opposing or adjacent wall at waist height

4 Lift second leg and place foot on wall above first, transferring weight onto hands.

5 Climb up wall using feet until body is straight and fully extended.

NB. Do not perform on a polished wooden staircase as this may lead to slippage of the hands, thus causing injury.

Door Wedge

Using a conventional door frame, lift body as high as possible, while wedging knees and back in the frame.

1 Stand sideways in a doorway with a sturdy door frame.

2 Grasp top lip of door frame with both hands.

3 Rest back flat against frame and put one foot on opposite side of frame at knee height.

4 Lift body using arms and position second foot above the first on the side of the frame.

5 Pull yourself up as high as possible whilst tucking in your knees and raising them as high as possible.

Floor Chicken

In a squatting position, place hands on floor with elbows bent, squeeze elbows with knees and lift feet off floor – and balance.

★★★☆☆

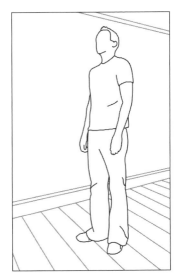

1 Find a clear, level floor space.

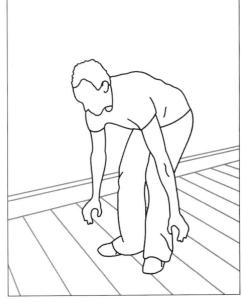

2 Place hands on floor and manoeuvre bent knees around outsides of arms, hooking them over the bent elbows.

3 Tilt body forward so weight is resting on elbows and feet are raised from the floor.

4 Hold position so as to create a state of equilibrium.

NB. This move can be performed as a challenge for multiple persons, called a Floor Chicken Face Off.

Intermediate

Brace

Place hands on a banister and lift legs as high as possible onto adjacent wall and lock into position.

1 Locate two banister uprights opposite a wall and stand on a step above the uprights.

2 Lean downwards and forwards, placing hands on tops of uprights.

3 Tense body and crouch down so as to transfer momentum when leaping the gap.

4 Swing across and transfer feet onto opposing wall.

5 Raise and spread feet as high as possible. Try and reach the ceiling.

NB. It can work in another way. Instead of using banisters for support you could use objects like a table or chest of drawers.

Enclosed Space Brace

A basic three-dimensional brace/wedge move performed in an enclosed space.

1 Locate yourself in a small-scale domestic water closet.

2 Stand on toilet seat and place hands on any surrounding surfaces in preparation for climb.

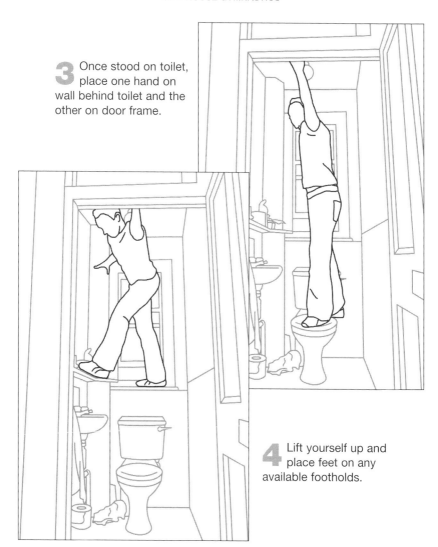

3 Once stood on toilet, place one hand on wall behind toilet and the other on door frame.

4 Lift yourself up and place feet on any available footholds.

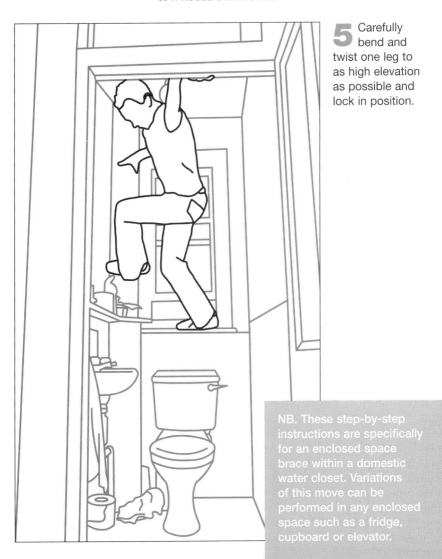

5 Carefully bend and twist one leg to as high elevation as possible and lock in position.

NB. These step-by-step instructions are specifically for an enclosed space brace within a domestic water closet. Variations of this move can be performed in any enclosed space such as a fridge, cupboard or elevator.

Upper Door Frame Grab

Grasp a thigh-high ledge with both hands and climb adjacent door frame with feet until the upper part of the frame is reached. Spread feet out to opposite corners of the door frame.

1 Stand between a doorway and window sill/radiator/banister/shelf.

2 Lean forward and grasp chosen ledge with both hands.

3 Place one foot on edge of door frame, at waist height.

4 Transfer weight onto hands and position second foot above first on door frame.

5 Climb up edge of doorway until top of door frame is reached. Place one foot in each corner.

NB. If performing this move barefoot, check door frame for splinters.

Jumping Jack Wedge

Using a space between two walls, jump up and lock feet and arms outwards, wedging yourself in a splayed position. Then climb up the space by jumping and locking in short bursts until you can't go any higher.

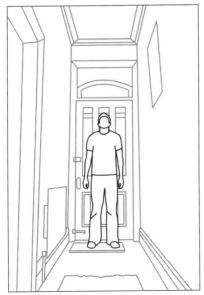

1 Stand in a corridor approximately one metre wide.

2 Spread arms wide and place hands on opposite walls at shoulder height.

3 Using arms for the initial push, jump upwards, locking feet outwards against walls so as to sustain an elevated position.

4 Repeat step three, jumping a bit higher up the wall each time.

5 Repeat step four until head touches ceiling.

NB. The greater the ceiling height, the more dramatic the aesthetic.

Extended Wedge

A close relation of the Door Wedge, but the space between the walls is wider and the legs must be stretched out straight, with the back wedged against the wall.

1 Stand in a corridor approximately one metre wide.

NB. If performing in a corridor where you could be obstructing a door, take extra care that your whereabouts are known.

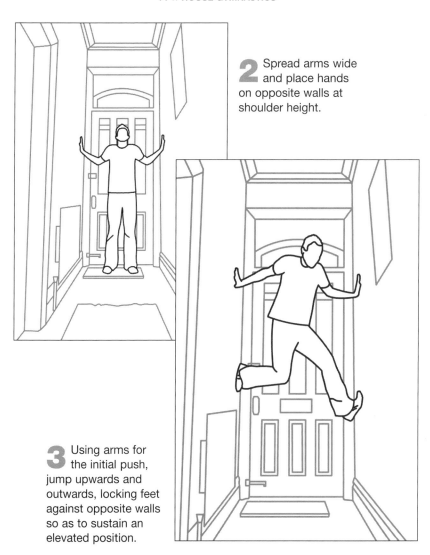

2 Spread arms wide and place hands on opposite walls at shoulder height.

3 Using arms for the initial push, jump upwards and outwards, locking feet against opposite walls so as to sustain an elevated position.

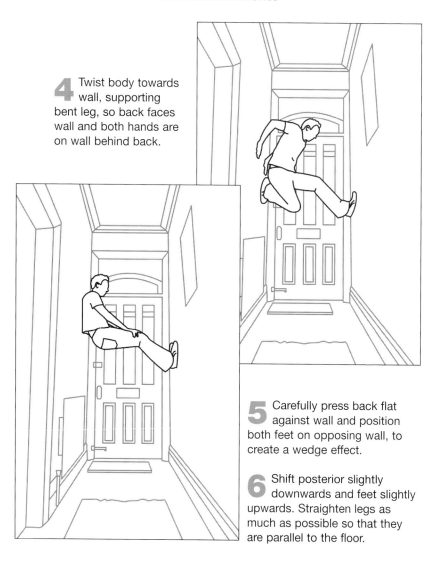

4 Twist body towards wall, supporting bent leg, so back faces wall and both hands are on wall behind back.

5 Carefully press back flat against wall and position both feet on opposing wall, to create a wedge effect.

6 Shift posterior slightly downwards and feet slightly upwards. Straighten legs as much as possible so that they are parallel to the floor.

Banister Snake

Holding onto banister rung, with body straight, raised from the floor and perpendicular to the banister spindles.

1 Crouch down at one end of a banister rail and grasp top of it with both hands.

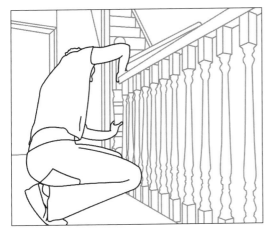

2 Twisting body, shift hands from a horizontal to a vertical position, locating them on the sturdy banister upright.

3 Straightening the legs and raising the leg closest to the banister, position it in the uppermost corner between upright and banister rail, on the furthest upright you can reach.

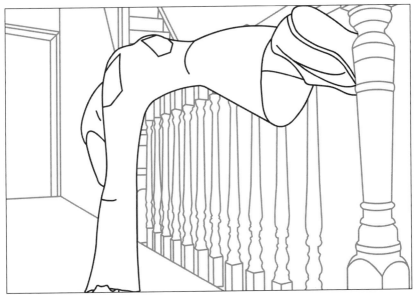

4 Move the second leg into position below the first, creating a wedge with the body.

5 Lower posterior so that body is completely straight and parallel to the banister rail.

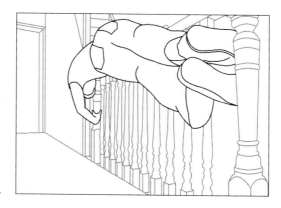

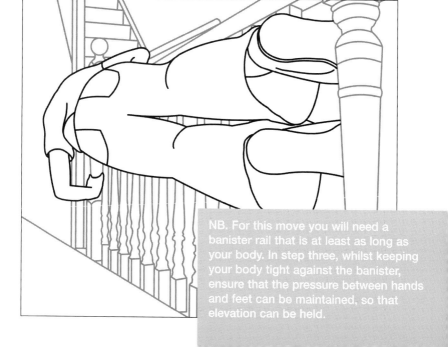

NB. For this move you will need a banister rail that is at least as long as your body. In step three, whilst keeping your body tight against the banister, ensure that the pressure between hands and feet can be maintained, so that elevation can be held.

The Triangle

Similar to a handstand but it must be performed on a banister or chest of drawers, with the body perfectly straight and feet high up on a wall, so as to create the shape of a right-angled triangle.

★★★★☆

1 Locate a rectangular elevated surface situated against a wall, such as a table or chest of drawers.

2 Grasp the top of the surface, with both hands at either side of the narrow edge furthest from the supporting wall.

3 Carefully climb up onto surface.

4 Kneel down, raise posterior high into the air and position head over the edge of the surface.

5 Transfer weight onto hands and place one foot onto wall.

6 Place second foot alongside first and climb up wall until body is completely straight, thus forming a triangle.

NB. Novices should begin with a triangle formation at ground level before attempting elevated surfaces.

Bath Urchin

Climb into the bath and place feet at the far end, either side of the taps. Brace the sides of the bath with both hands, push upwards and arch your back.

★ ★ ★ ★ ☆

1 Crouch in the centre of a standard bath, facing the taps.

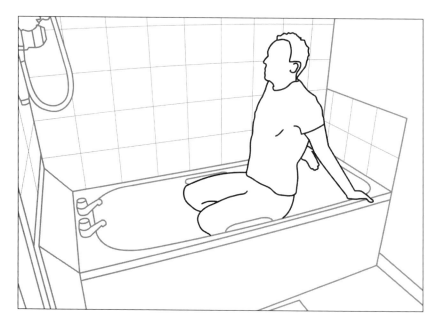

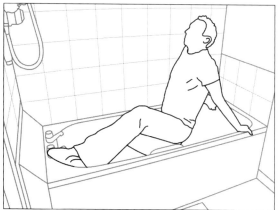

2 Move arms backwards, placing on hands on edges of bath.

3 Position left foot to the left of left tap.

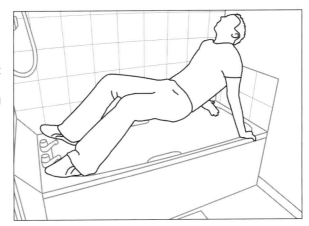

4 Place right foot to the right of right tap, thus lifting posterior from the bottom of bath.

5 Raise groin and tilt head backwards, thus forming an arch that mirrors the internal curvature of the bath.

NB. This was the first ever move to incorporate the bath. Do not attempt this move if the bath is filled with water as this may lead to death by drowning.

Chair Chicken

Climb onto a sturdy and stable chair, and stand up, facing outwards. Placing hands on either arm of the chair, lock knees around elbows and lean further forwards, raising your feet from the chair.

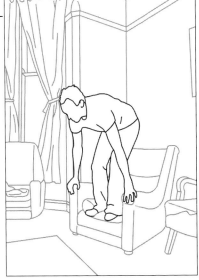

1 Find a conventional armchair and stand in front of it, with your back to the chair.

2 Climb onto chair and bend forwards, placing hands on arm rests.

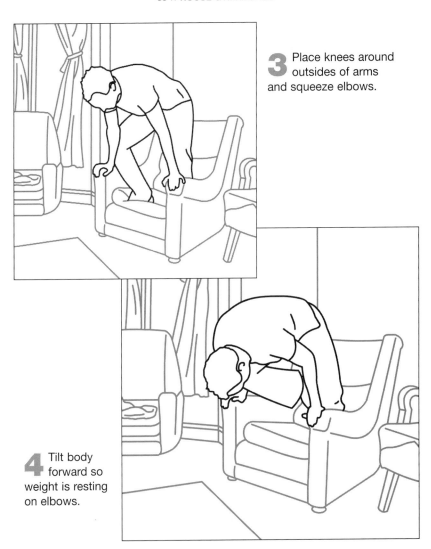

3 Place knees around outsides of arms and squeeze elbows.

4 Tilt body forward so weight is resting on elbows.

5 Rock body forward until feet are raised from the chair. Hold position so as to create a state of equilibrium.

NB. This move is the more challenging version of the Floor Chicken, which appeared in the Beginner chapter.

Ceiling Walk

A slightly easier version of the Ceiling Stand in the Expert chapter, this move is performed with one foot on ceiling and one foot on the wall, with body vertical.

1 Locate a sturdy banister upright, situated adjacent to a wall and with ceiling approximately five to six feet above the top of banister.

2 Place preferred hand onto sphere of banister upright.

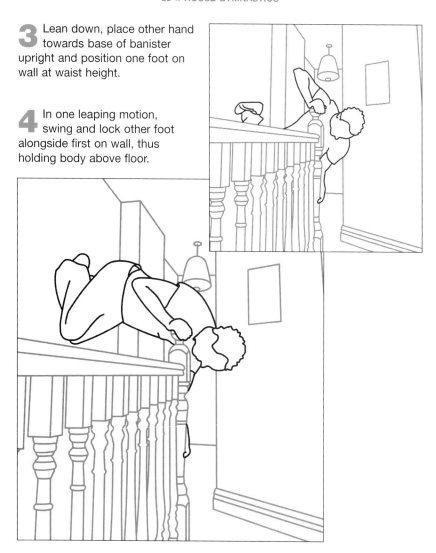

3 Lean down, place other hand towards base of banister upright and position one foot on wall at waist height.

4 In one leaping motion, swing and lock other foot alongside first on wall, thus holding body above floor.

5 Slowly walk backwards up wall until you reach the ceiling.

6 Place one foot where ceiling meets the wall and the other on the ceiling, and lock in position so as to take on the appearance of walking.

NB. Make sure that the walls are free from objects that you could break or injure yourself on during dismount.

Y Chromosome

Using a support, such as a banister upright, use feet to climb up two facing walls and then fully extend and straighten legs, so as to form the shape of the letter Y.

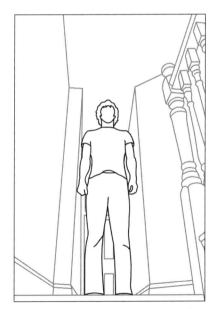

1 Stand between two facing walls that are about a metre apart, and with a support within arms reach in front of you.

2 Lean forwards placing one hand on sphere of banister upright and other hand lower down on the banister upright.

3 Raise one leg and position foot on one of the opposing walls at approximately the height of the banister sphere.

4 Position second foot on the other opposing wall at the same height, thus forming a Y-shape from a worm's eye view.

NB. Concentrate on keeping body straight and level to the floor. If unsure how parallel you are, ask your spotting partner to place a spirit level on your back.

Expert

Free-Standing Suspension Bridge (FSSB)

This move requires two people with an acute sense of balance. One person must grasp the hands of the other, then use their feet to climb up the legs of the supporting person, leaning backwards to complete the move.

★★★★★

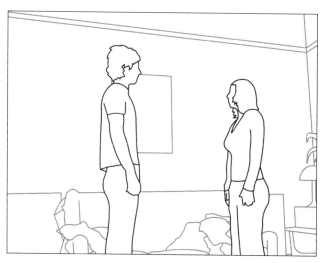

1 Stand facing a fellow House Gymnast, one metre apart.

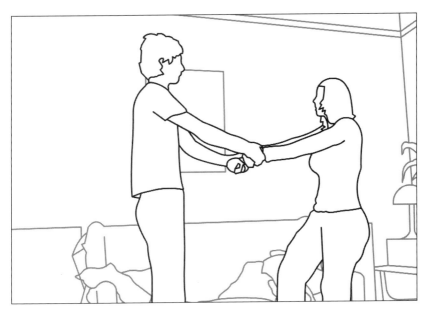

2 The person who will become the solid foundation should grasp the other person's hands.

3 The climber must now place one foot on one thigh of the supporting person.

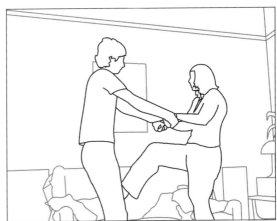

4 The climber now places their other foot on the other thigh of the supporter and pulls themselves up so that all their weight is now on the thighs of the supporter.

5 The supporter leans back whilst the climber straightens their legs and leans back in the opposite direction, creating a state of equilibrium.

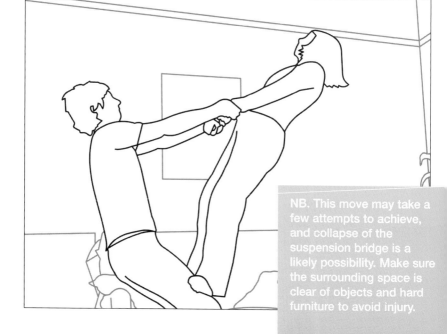

NB. This move may take a few attempts to achieve, and collapse of the suspension bridge is a likely possibility. Make sure the surrounding space is clear of objects and hard furniture to avoid injury.

Carpet Crab

Put arms underneath knees and lift all of body weight from the floor so as to create the illusion of a crab.

★ ★ ★ ★ ★

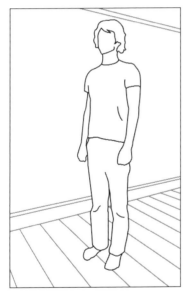

1 Find a clear, level floor space and stand with feet apart.

2 Bend forward, lowering hands between legs towards floor.

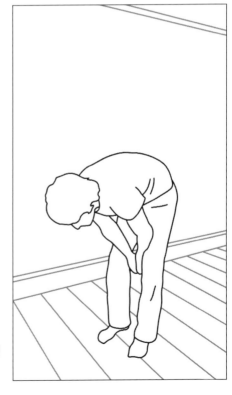

3 Place hands on floor behind and bending knees, hook knees over elbows.

4 Balance weight of legs on upper arms and rock slowly backwards raising feet from floor. When balanced, hold position.

NB. The carpet crab is arguably the most difficult House Gymnastics move. Even though it's not as dangerous or strenuous as the xXx (see page 122), it requires extreme flexibility, suppleness, balance and strength.

Elevated Carpet Crab

The Carpet Crab manoeuvre elevated from the floor via an elevated surface/object such as a chair.

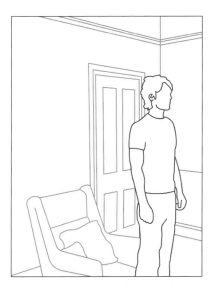

1 Find a conventional armchair and stand in front of it, with your back to the chair.

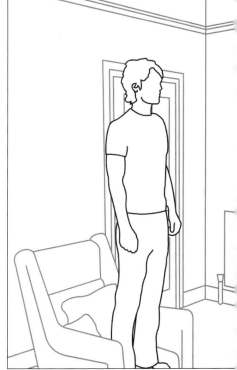

2 Climb onto chair.

3 Lean down, putting arms between legs, bending knees and placing hands on armrests.

NB. Beginners should place some pillows on the floor in front of chair to cushion potential falls. The more advanced and flexible can make the move more aesthetically pleasing by bringing soles of feet together in a praying position in the final move.

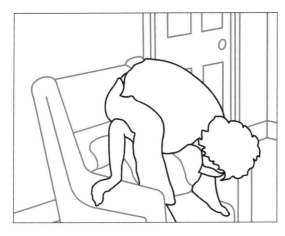

4 Bend forwards and hook knees over elbows.

5 Balance weight of legs on upper arms and rock slowly backwards, raising feet from chair. When balanced, hold position.

Armchair Handstand

*Perform a handstand with hands on each arm
of the chair and feet on wall behind chair.*

★ ★ ★ ★ ★

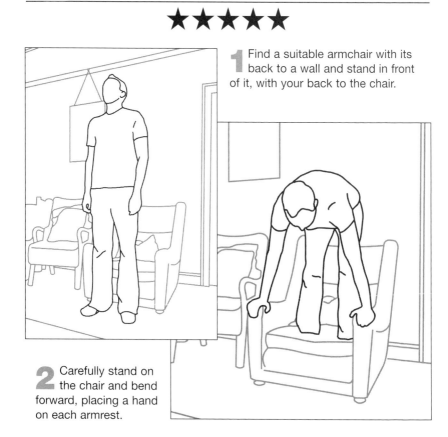

1 Find a suitable armchair with its back to a wall and stand in front of it, with your back to the chair.

2 Carefully stand on the chair and bend forward, placing a hand on each armrest.

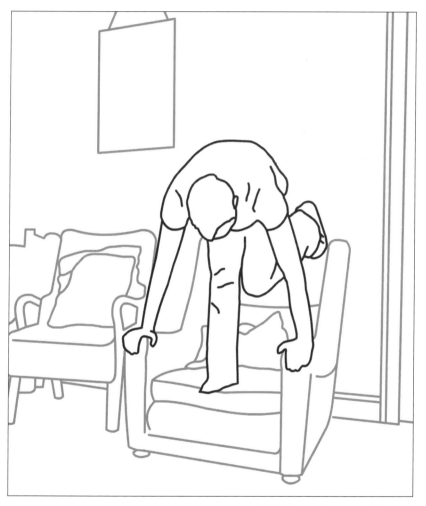

3 Lift one foot onto the top edge of the headrest area.

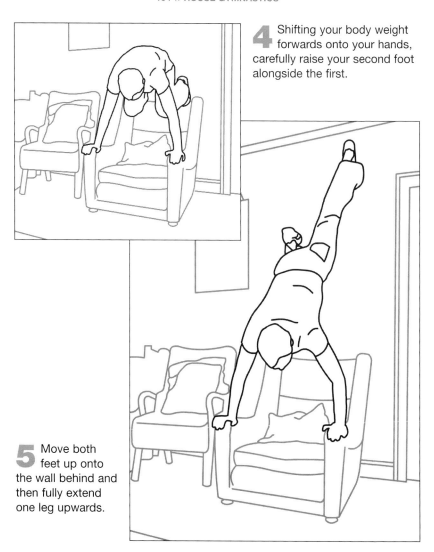

4 Shifting your body weight forwards onto your hands, carefully raise your second foot alongside the first.

5 Move both feet up onto the wall behind and then fully extend one leg upwards.

6 Fully extend the other leg and make sure that your body is straight and fully extended.

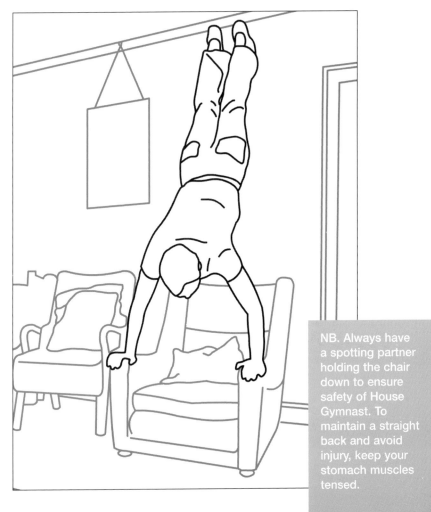

NB. Always have a spotting partner holding the chair down to ensure safety of House Gymnast. To maintain a straight back and avoid injury, keep your stomach muscles tensed.

One-Handed Starfish

*This is similar to the basic Brace move, but the
legs are positioned across an open space and arms
are spread out to form a star shape. One hand
is then raised in the air for three seconds.*

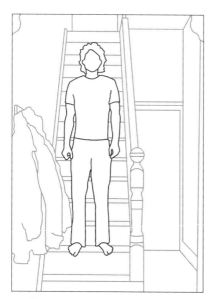

1 Stand on bottom step of stairs facing away from the staircase.

2 Place one hand on sphere of banister and the other hand on coat rail (or similar support).

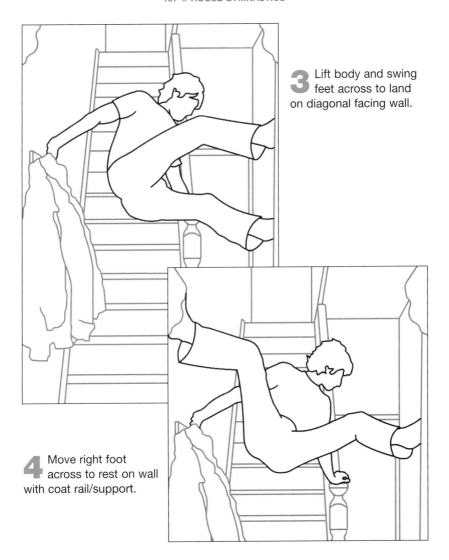

3 Lift body and swing feet across to land on diagonal facing wall.

4 Move right foot across to rest on wall with coat rail/support.

5 Push up on banister sphere, raise and twist body whilst releasing hand from coat rail. Hold hand above head for three seconds.

NB. This move requires a very specific set of structures but a very similar move can be achieved using other areas of the house.

X-door

Perform a basic handstand in a conventional doorway and then move hands and feet to the corners of the door frame, thus creating an X-shape.

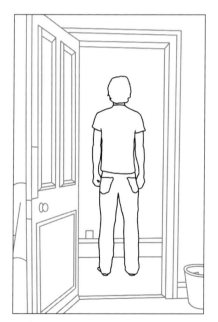

1 Stand outside the doorway to a room, as if you have just left it.

2 Lean forwards and place hands on floor, a shoulder-width apart, approximately 50cm from doorway.

3 Place one foot onto door frame at waist height.

4 Transfer weight onto hands and raise second foot onto the other side of the doorframe.

5 Climb up door frame with feet until upper corners are reached.

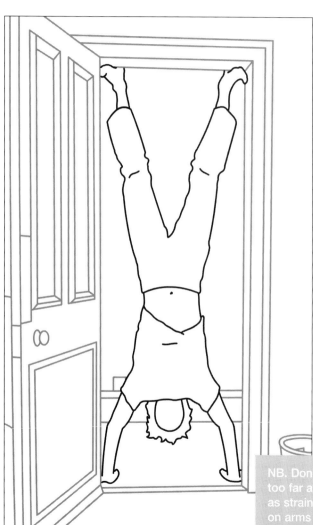

6 Walk hands towards the door frame and when you reach it, place hands into the bottom corners.

NB. Don't start this move too far away from doorway as strain of body weight on arms will sap energy before move is complete.

Spiderman

*Climb up as high as possible into the corner/alcove
of a room or corridor and wedge body into position,
with one foot in the highest corner.*

★ ★ ★ ★ ★

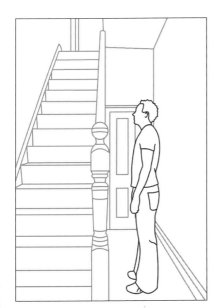

1 Locate yourself at the side of a staircase, facing sturdy banisters with a handrail with a gradient of approximately 45 degrees.

2 Grasp handrail with both hands and put one foot on a step, in space between banister spindles.

3 Raise body using arms and climb the outside of the banisters.

4 Moving feet between banister spindles, make your way to where the banister meets the ceiling/wall.

5 Place feet on any available ledge, such as a door frame.

6 Raise one foot into uppermost corner of the alcove.

NB. Strong arm muscles are required for this move and a spotting partner is essential.

Ceiling Stand

*Using a banister for support, raise legs
into the air and place both feet on the ceiling.
Lock into position, keeping body vertical.*

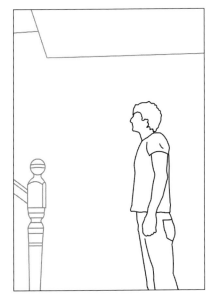

1 Locate a sturdy banister upright, adjacent to a wall and with ceiling height approximately five to six feet above the top of banister.

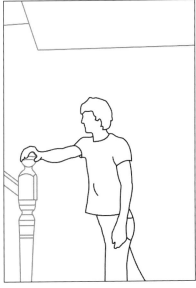

2 Place hand nearest wall onto sphere of banister.

3 Lean down and place other hand towards base of banister upright and position one foot on wall at waist height.

NB. In reference to step five, if ceiling cannot be located with the first foot do not attempt step six as you could overbalance, fall and seriously injure yourself.

4 In one leaping motion lock other foot alongside first on wall thus holding body above floor.

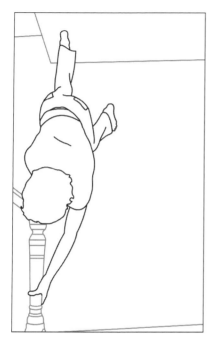

5 Slowly walk up wall and carefully locate ceiling with one foot.

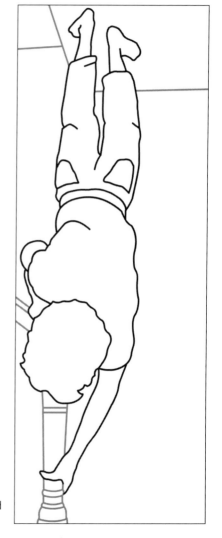

6 Place both feet onto ceiling and ensure that body is perfectly straight and in line with banister upright.

Human Flag

Using a sturdy pole and an adjoining surface (such as a table), and an adjacent wall, raise body up to an elevation of 90 degrees. Lock in position so as to take on the appearance of a flag.

★ ★ ★ ★ ★

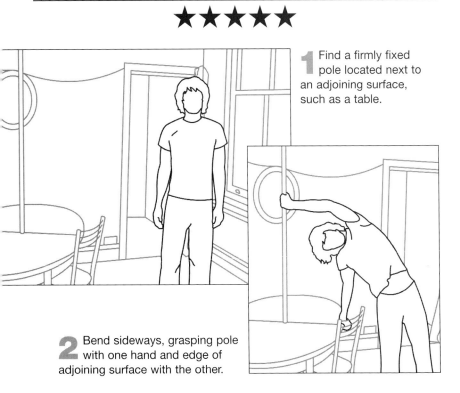

1 Find a firmly fixed pole located next to an adjoining surface, such as a table.

2 Bend sideways, grasping pole with one hand and edge of adjoining surface with the other.

3 Raise leg nearest wall into the air and place foot on wall. Move other foot alongside.

NB. This move can also be performed on a pole without an adjoining surface (such as a lamppost) but the aesthetic will be of a poorer quality.

4 Transfer body weight onto surface and use pole to pull legs upwards so that they are perpendicular to the pole, thus turning you into a Human Flag.

xXx

The 'Holy Grail' of House Gymnastics. Using various wedge and brace methods, climb up to the ceiling in an alcove and splay yourself against the ceiling, spreading arms and legs out as far as they will go.

1 Find a corridor space approximately as wide as you are tall. Any additional supports in the area could aid elevation.

2 Place one hand on a support (if needed) and prepare yourself.

3 Carefully lean forward and press other hand flat against wall.

4 Position foot on wall behind.

5 Taking the strain on your arms, wedge other foot alongside first.

NB. Clearly the xXx is highly dangerous and a number of spotting partners are strongly recommended, as well as trained first-aiders. The dismount is the most dangerous part of this move so take extra care.

6 Finally, shift remaining hand onto opposing wall and climb up walls until back is flat against ceiling.

Practical Applications

Now that you've learned the moves, take House Gymnastics into your life. Not just for fun or fitness, it can be applied and adapted to assist in many practical household chores.

The Jumping Jack Wedge (see page 67) is ideal for such tricky household maintenance tasks as dusting high corners, hanging Christmas decorations, installing cabling or doing a bit of painting to cover up those nasty marks left on the walls after a House Gymnastics session.

The Jumping Jack Wedge comes into play again when dusting the high corner of a room.

NB. As with the practical use of the Jumping Jack Wedge, a spotting partner is essential for passing brushes, feather dusters etc. once the House Gymnast is in position. Having a spotting partner to direct you to cobwebs or an area to paint can make things much easier, as widerange visibility is usually better from the ground. As always, though, a spotting partner is primarily there for safety.

Installing a blind
using a Shelf
Pirouette.

The Shelf Pirouette (see page 34) is quite a versatile move. As well as putting up blinds, it can be used to paint the top of a window frame, or install high shelving. When used to lean into a room, the Shelf Pirouette can be used to remove cobwebs and even for a little light painting.

As an added practical application, preparation for a Fridge Enclosed Space Brace is a perfect excuse to clean the fridge and remove rotten/mouldy food. And it is advisable to clean the toilet bowl for a WC Enclosed Space Brace, in case you fall into it and catch a faeces-related disease. Thus House Gymnastics becomes a sanitary catalyst.

Let's not forget that while House Gymnastics can be an added incentive to get those chores done, it can also create them. Here's how to put things right after you've stacked it.

How to repair a broken coat rail

When a coat rail comes away from the wall and falls down, it is often the result of one too many One-Handed Starfish manoeuvres in the

hallway. It can be easily repaired with some plaster, a sturdy screw and a drill. If you are fed up with hanging your coats on the floor, follow the steps below:

- If needed, buy a new coat rail.
- Pull out broken Rawlplug and debris from hole.
- Fill hole with filler/plaster.
- Allow to dry overnight.
- Carefully align drill and drill a new hole in the plaster.
- Fit a new Rawlplug and screw coat rail into position.

How to cover up wall marks

Trainers and shoes often leave marks on walls: Jumping Jack Wedges and Ceiling Stands are public enemy number one. If you find your walls covered in dirt and scuff marks, follow the instructions below:

- Try wiping away the marks with a cloth and surface cleaner.
- If this fails, try a layer of paint applied with either a brush or roller.
- If the mark still shows through, cover it with a layer of sealant or PVA glue before applying another layer of paint.
- If all else fails, wallpaper the entire wall and use the excuse that 'the room needed a change'.

Moving On

House Gymnastics is a vibrant and organic art-form, so once you've mastered the basic moves, start inventing your own.

Move of the Month

Move of the Month is a monthly competition set up by Harrison and Ford to encourage pro-activity within the House Gymnastics community, as a way of developing ever more exciting, interesting and difficult moves.

To win Move of the Month, you have to submit a 100 per cent real photo of yourself doing your own patented House Gymnastics move, or performing an extreme or synchronized version of an existing Harrison and Ford manoeuvre. The best move will be chosen each month and is judged on creativity, style and difficulty. The winner's name and photo will be displayed on the website and if a new move is created, it will be logged and acknowledged. Previous winners include

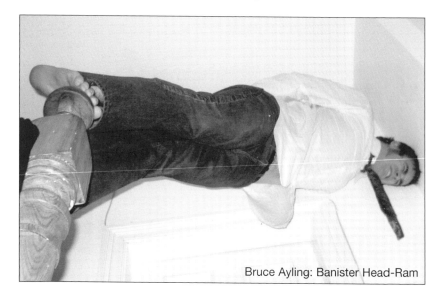

Bruce Ayling: Banister Head-Ram

Steve Ray: Human Flag

Bruce Ayling for his very painful and difficult Banister Head-Ram (opposite below) and Steve Ray in December 2002 for his extraordinary Human Flag (see page 120). The Human Flag requires a particular kind of desk/structure, as you can see in the image, and super-human upper-body strength.

Move of the Month rules

● Moves must be inventive and held in position for at least 3 seconds.

● They must be documented, using either a digital photograph, print or video footage. All images will be examined thoroughly to eliminate fraudulent submissions.

● The documentation can be submitted via e-mail, website or post.

● The name of the move is an important aspect, as well as the location and difficulty.

Move of the Month: Anwar Hoogland
Back Door Bat Hang

1 Locate a pair of industrial double doors and stand facing the opposite direction to which the doors open.

2 Position the doors at an angle of 45 degrees, twist your arms backwards and place a hand on the top edge of each door.

3 Lift yourself up, raising feet to the top of the door frame.

4 Walk up the wall until your legs are straight and then lower your head towards the ground, looking outwards.

Move of the Month: Sharmila Cogger
Set Square

1 Find a clear, level floor space.

2 Lean forwards and place hands and head on floor in preparation for a headstand (use a pillow to cushion your head if performing this move on a hard floor).

3 Raise legs into a standard headstand position, so that your whole body is straight up in the air.

4 Using great muscle control, slowly lower legs 90 degrees and lock in a right-angled position.

Site Specific

Site specific House Gymnastics originated when Ford chose to bust a daring move on the large fibreglass goose that takes pride of place on the traffic island near Forest Fields recreation ground in Nottingham. The goose is in place every year during the first week of October and heralds the start of the traditional Nottingham Goose Fair. This daring stunt took House Gymnastics into an exciting new arena, as well as bestowing Ford with his first serious injury. It meant that House Gymnastics could offer unique and once-in-a-lifetime opportunities that could only happen in specific locations at certain times. Hence

The Goose

Double Tate Brace

Banister Tate Snake

'The Goose' is a move that can only be recreated on the actual Nottingham Goose when it is in place on the island.

When you've mastered the moves inside the confines of your house, take it a step further by practising your skills on location.

Car Monkey

Outcrop-Rock Handstand

Board Room Inverted Hang

Office Moves

The office is a very popular location for many House Gymnasts to bust some moves. The office can be quite a boring, stifling place and House Gymnastics brings a sense of dynamism and physicality. In fact, House Gymnastics has been shown to actually increase the creativity and energy levels of office participants, which can't be a bad thing for business.

As always, take care not to damage your surroundings or yourself, as this could result in dismissal in the former case and costly time off work with the latter.

The office space affords the House Gymnast a new wide range of possibilities when busting moves. Large desks, computer equipment, photocopiers and coffee machines all encourage creative manoeuvres. Steve Ray's Move of the Month-winning Human Flag was performed in his workplace (see page 137). In the bland working environment of the office, House Gymnastics can be used as an icebreaker for new employees, or bonding sessions for existing workers. The image on the previous spread is of keen office House Gymnast Matt Patterson. When bored with the daily routine and rigmarole of office duties, he likes to slip away to the boardroom and hang from the rafters.

Here are some tips for the House Gymnast performing office moves.

- It is advisable to remove shoes, as they offer a lot less grip than trainers; a loss of friction can result in a fall.
- If you are wearing a necktie, it is advisable to tuck it out of the way, although if you are documenting the move a loose tie can give a good indication of body angle for the remote viewer.
- Depending on your boss, it is advisable to be fairly discreet when busting moves.
- Remember to record your moves as they will act as a guide and inspiration to others performing office moves.

Synchronized Moves

In House Gymnastics terms, a synchronized move involves two or more House Gymnasts performing exactly the same move in the same architectural area. The moves do not have to be exactly symmetrical, but this does make the synchronization more aesthetically pleasing. If there

is a large group of House Gymnasts feeling particularly subversive, they could attempt Undercover Floor Chickens. This is a mass synchronized move that can be used to surprise onlookers in a public space such as a bar, shopping centre or museum. Around 20 people, evenly dispersed within the public area, are needed for the performance to be effective. Invent a secret sign or noise at which everyone will try to perform Floor Chickens (see page 55) for 20–30 seconds. They will then walk away and go about their business as if nothing had happened, baffling onlookers.

Combination Moves

Combination moves are different from synchronized ones in that they combine different House Gymnastics positions, by multiple participants, in the same architectural area. Combination moves are great to perform amongst a large group of friends as you can inspire each other and create large, innovative accumulations of House Gymnastics shapes.

Exchange Visits

Exchanges involve a visit to the domestic space of another House Gymnast. The idea of exchange visits is to increase communication and provide a social aspect to the sport. These can be informal or formal visits, where new moves and tips can be exchanged between the participants. It gives each House Gymnast a chance to test their agility and skills in a new arena. The goal is to build up a network of exchange arenas so that participants can get to know fellow members from around the globe.

Exchange visits can be between individuals or groups and, because House Gymnastics has members all over the world, exchanges can involve travel to foreign countries. With an exchange visit, members can build bonds with other House Gymnasts and get inspiration from new surroundings and feedback from fellow enthusiasts. A House Gymnast would usually look for other members in his or her area first and arrange an exchange via e-mail, before attempting international travel.

Remember to bring lots of film and, if you are using a digital camera, batteries for documenting moves during the exchange visit. There's nothing worse than your camera dying just as you bust that contender for Move of the Month! When taking part in an exchange visit, it is important to observe the same House Gymnastics safety rules as you would in your own home, so check things like banisters for sturdiness and be aware of spatial differences. Moves that are easy in your own home could be difficult in new surroundings due to differences in layout and size (for example, ceiling height and corridor width). On the other hand, moves that are normally difficult to perform at home might become a lot easier when performed during an

Guidelines for Exchanges

- Only organise exchanges with friends or certified House Gymnastics members from the website.

- If in doubt, consult Harrison and Ford via the website.

- If you are taking part in a foreign exchange, make sure you get all the appropriate vaccinations and remember your passport.

- Initial contact should be made by e-mail and phone – do not give out your home address straight away.

- Meet up for a chat/coffee in a neutral location beforehand to discuss the exchange.

- Check that the person you do an exchange with does not have any criminal convictions and is of sound mind.

- If the exchange is agreed, be prepared to document all moves performed and details of the person, his address, etc.

- When in another member's home, it is polite to remove shoes to avoid marking walls or damaging fixtures and fittings.

- And finally, always tell a friend or relative of your whereabouts.

exchange. For example, the ceiling stand that is impossible in your own home could now become possible due to a lower ceiling in the exchange environment.

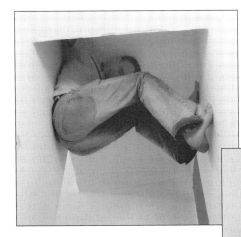

Member Number: 001
Visitor: James Ford
Host Address: 115 Waterloo Crescent, Radford, Nottingham
Host: Bruce Ayling
Date of visit: 10/11/02
Move performed: Wedge

Member Number: 005
Visitor: Bruce Ayling
Host Address: 12 Wiverton Road, Sherwood Rise, Nottingham
Host: Harrison and Ford
Date of visit: 29/11/02
Move performed: Banister Headram

House Gymnastics Challenges

7 Eleven

This challenge is useful as a training exercise and as an introduction to the more difficult challenges. To complete it successfully, 11 moves must be performed in seven minutes. The domestic space to be used should be examined beforehand to determine which moves can be performed. The challenger then picks 11 moves randomly out of a hat. If competing with other House Gymnasts, the person who completes the most moves or in the fastest time wins.

Floor Chicken Face-Off

This challenge can be performed as a face-off between two people (as shown in the photograph) or as a group event (as with Undercover

Rules and notes

- Perform the contest on level flooring.

- Be careful that participants are not too close together as head-butting could occur.

- Make sure participants are situated on the same type of surface (i.e. don't have one on a carpet and one on a wooden floor).

- The Floor Chicken must be performed as dictated in the step-by-step instructions on page ??, no variations are allowed.

- Unbiased adjudicators should be present to check the individual moves for validity and time duration.

- If neither participant has managed to perform a valid Floor Chicken within five minutes, the contest is considered a draw and both people are made fun of.

Floor Chickens on page 147). The rules are simple: the first person to perform a Floor Chicken and hold the position for three seconds wins. With multiple participants, the event could be split into knockout rounds with a grand final to determine the overall winner.

The 25th Element

The 25th Element is a special endurance performance, invented as a challenge with exchange visit or group possibilities. It involves two people performing all 25 classic Harrison and Ford moves, in a tag-team fashion in 25 minutes. Each move has to be performed in its appropriate place around the home, i.e. you can't do all 25 moves in one room. The moves must be completed in alphabetical order and each person must complete the move before moving on to the next. Harrison and Ford failed on their first attempt on 7 December 2002 (which was recorded for the exhibition DVD) mainly due to Ford's hungover state, and his inability to perform carpet crabs and handstands. Harrison and Ford managed to complete 24.5 moves in 26 minutes. The anguish in the film is intense and there is an overt element of pathos when Ford continually struggles and fails to perform the Elevated Carpet Crab. The viewer becomes part of the entourage following Harrison and Ford around the house, willing them to succeed. People connect with House Gymnastics and The 25th Element in particular because it's all about real enthusiasm, emotion and, in this case, failure. Everyone connects with failure. But the failure of Harrison and Ford to complete their own challenge may inspire others to take it upon themselves to attempt the task.

NB. For documentation purposes of potential challengers, the performance must be video-recorded in one continuous shot (use the onscreen time display on the camera to show duration). It must be timed and adjudicated by an unbiased third party, who must sign and date a certified checklist of the 25 moves.

The Twelve Point Five

For this challenge the same rules apply as for The 25th Element, except it is performed by a single person and the 25 moves must be completed in 12.5 minutes. The FSSB move is replaced with the Bath Urchin. The first attempt at this challenge was successfully made by Ford on 21 May 2003, who completed it in 11 minutes and 53 seconds.

The Ten Commandments

Ten people form ephemeral human sculptures as they attempt to complete the Ten Commandments as set by Harrison and Ford, in ten minutes.

You will need: two groups of ten people, ten minutes, one corridor space, one bath, and an armchair and table.

Volunteers take it in turns to perform moves. Each member of a group should be stationed in the appropriate parts of the room to perform

The Ten Commandments

- Bath Urchin
- Bridge
- Door Wedge
- Elevated Carpet Crab
- Floor Chicken
- Jumping Jack Wedge
- Shelf Pirouette
- The Triangle
- Upper Door Frame Grab
- X-door

NB. House Gymnasts may use different apparatus and perform different moves if they wish, but there must be at least three five-star moves and five three-star moves that utilise different body muscles and strengths in the selection chosen.

NB. Ten adjudicators need to be present to check the individual moves for validity and time duration.

a move each. They should all perform their allotted move simultaneously. Each move must be held for three seconds. Once everyone has completed their move, they move on to the next House Gymnastics space to perform a different move, thus evoking memories of circuit training classes and school gym lessons.

Approximately one minute is allocated for each move. Even if someone doesn't complete the move, they progress to the next. Each group should receive a mark out of 100 because the maximum number of completed moves by the ten people is 100. So if everyone performs nine out of the ten moves, their group total will be 90. Set up a league table to see which group achieves the highest total in the quickest time.

The xXx Challenge

The xXx is a move designed for the more experienced, skilled and fearless House Gymnast. Only attempt this challenge if you can perform all the other moves. The perfect xXx has so far eluded even Harrison and Ford and is the ultimate House Gymnastics challenge. Tim Cleary (member 008) broke his wrist trying to perform an xXx in November 2002 and needed surgery to reattach his tendons. Whoever manages to perform an xXx will receive a poorly designed, low-quality certificate signed by Harrison and Ford. Images and video footage will be thoroughly examined to eliminate fraudulent submissions.

xXx submissions are judged and graded on width of space (relative to the person), height, location, and straightness and splayed-ness of the body. Obviously the move is more impressive if attempted in a public space with onlookers present, as this adds pressure to the performance. The House Gymnast will be laughed at by the crowd if he fails miserably. However, the presence of a crowd can also be an advantage as their cheering can spur the person on and, if serious injury occurs, there will be lots of people around to call an ambulance.

Jason Godbold Smith produced this first-ever attempt at an xXx in Nottingham on 29 November 2002, whilst dressed as John Travolta. Unfortunately his feet are too low and his back is not pressed against the ceiling. However, Jason has certainly thrown down the gauntlet.

Level of achievement = 8/10

Steve Ray from Dallas, Texas, USA busted this xXx attempt on 16 December 2002, in the corridor of the office building where he works. Steve is an avid House Gymnast and Harrison and Ford were impressed by his one-handed bravery. However, the corridor is too narrow to per-

form a fully-fledged xXx, which is why Steve's legs are bent and too low down on the wall. Harrison and Ford were also sceptical about whether this move was held for three seconds.

Level of achievement = 7/10

This is an excellent xXx attempt by Chris Fellowes from Wokingham, England on 21 March 2003. It warrants a 9.5/10 due to the sheer width of the space and because his legs are fully extended. His back is against the ceiling but to achieve a 10/10, his legs need to be higher up.

Level of achievement = 9.5/10

COMING SOON

*House Jim and House Spanks the inflatable dolls –
exact replicas of the founders of House Gymnastics.
Manoeuvre them into any position and stick them
around your house using the supplied velcro.
(May require additional blowing to keep them up.)*

About the authors

James Ford

James Ford is a video/installation artist and web designer. His work attempts to imbue banality with new meaning, and to entice the viewer into trying the tasks and projects that he sets himself, thus blurring the definition of artist and viewer and questioning the nature of authorship. His artworks take many forms, ranging from a ball of bogies in a broken eggcup and photographs of number-plates bearing his initials, to a film documentary about warts. He currently lives in London and spends too much time at his computer.

Spencer Harrison

Spencer Harrison is a Mancunian photographer/ filmmaker who likes to collect vintage pin-up magazines and swim in the ocean whenever he gets the chance. Harrison hopes to tour around Australia on a motorbike, meeting House Gymnastics members along the way and eating wichetty grubs whilst documenting his travels. He currently spends his time between Manchester, Nottingham and London.

Visit www.housegymnastics.com for more information, images, music and camaraderie.